Dear God,
today I am thankful for...

A 5-year gratitude journal

Keep Track Books

God is good — and worthy to be praised!

*With the help of this gratitude journal
you can record your thankfulness daily
and be reminded of how good God is.*

*As you fill in the journal and return to view
the pages later, you will see how amazing God is
and how many blessings there are in your life.*

*To get started, go to today's date,
jot down the current year and write down
the thing(s) – big or small – that you're
thankful for today.*

May God bless you!

CreateSpace, Charleston SC
Design © Keep Track Books

January 1

Dear God, today I am thankful for...　| 20 ___

Dear God, today I am thankful for...　| 20 ___

Dear God, today I am thankful for...　| 20 ___

Dear God, today I am thankful for...　| 20 ___

Dear God, today I am thankful for...　| 20 ___

January 2

Dear God, today I am thankful for...	20 ___

Dear God, today I am thankful for...	20 ___

Dear God, today I am thankful for...	20 ___

Dear God, today I am thankful for...	20 ___

Dear God, today I am thankful for...	20 ___

January 3

Dear God, today I am thankful for...   20 ___

Dear God, today I am thankful for...   20 ___

Dear God, today I am thankful for...   20 ___

Dear God, today I am thankful for...   20 ___

Dear God, today I am thankful for...   20 ___

January 4

Dear God, today I am thankful for...   20 ___

Dear God, today I am thankful for...   20 ___

Dear God, today I am thankful for...   20 ___

Dear God, today I am thankful for...   20 ___

Dear God, today I am thankful for...   20 ___

January 5

Dear God, today I am thankful for... | 20 ___

Dear God, today I am thankful for... | 20 ___

Dear God, today I am thankful for... | 20 ___

Dear God, today I am thankful for... | 20 ___

Dear God, today I am thankful for... | 20 ___

January 6

Dear God, today I am thankful for...　20 ___

Dear God, today I am thankful for...　20 ___

Dear God, today I am thankful for...　20 ___

Dear God, today I am thankful for...　20 ___

Dear God, today I am thankful for...　20 ___

January 7

Dear God, today I am thankful for... | 20 ___

Dear God, today I am thankful for... | 20 ___

Dear God, today I am thankful for... | 20 ___

Dear God, today I am thankful for... | 20 ___

Dear God, today I am thankful for... | 20 ___

January 8

Dear God, today I am thankful for... | 20 ___

Dear God, today I am thankful for... | 20 ___

Dear God, today I am thankful for... | 20 ___

Dear God, today I am thankful for... | 20 ___

Dear God, today I am thankful for... | 20 ___

January 9

| Dear God, today I am thankful for... | 20 ___ |

| Dear God, today I am thankful for... | 20 ___ |

| Dear God, today I am thankful for... | 20 ___ |

| Dear God, today I am thankful for... | 20 ___ |

| Dear God, today I am thankful for... | 20 ___ |

January 10

Dear God, today I am thankful for...	20 ___

Dear God, today I am thankful for...	20 ___

Dear God, today I am thankful for...	20 ___

Dear God, today I am thankful for...	20 ___

Dear God, today I am thankful for...	20 ___

January 11

Dear God, today I am thankful for...	20 ___

Dear God, today I am thankful for...	20 ___

Dear God, today I am thankful for...	20 ___

Dear God, today I am thankful for...	20 ___

Dear God, today I am thankful for...	20 ___

January 12

Dear God, today I am thankful for...	20 ___

Dear God, today I am thankful for...	20 ___

Dear God, today I am thankful for...	20 ___

Dear God, today I am thankful for...	20 ___

Dear God, today I am thankful for...	20 ___

January 13

Dear God, today I am thankful for...   20 ___

Dear God, today I am thankful for...   20 ___

Dear God, today I am thankful for...   20 ___

Dear God, today I am thankful for...   20 ___

Dear God, today I am thankful for...   20 ___

January 14

| Dear God, today I am thankful for... | 20 ___ |

| Dear God, today I am thankful for... | 20 ___ |

| Dear God, today I am thankful for... | 20 ___ |

| Dear God, today I am thankful for... | 20 ___ |

| Dear God, today I am thankful for... | 20 ___ |

January 15

Dear God, today I am thankful for…	20 ___

Dear God, today I am thankful for…	20 ___

Dear God, today I am thankful for…	20 ___

Dear God, today I am thankful for…	20 ___

Dear God, today I am thankful for…	20 ___

January 16

Dear God, today I am thankful for... | 20 ___

Dear God, today I am thankful for... | 20 ___

Dear God, today I am thankful for... | 20 ___

Dear God, today I am thankful for... | 20 ___

Dear God, today I am thankful for... | 20 ___

January 17

Dear God, today I am thankful for...	20 ___

Dear God, today I am thankful for...	20 ___

Dear God, today I am thankful for...	20 ___

Dear God, today I am thankful for...	20 ___

Dear God, today I am thankful for...	20 ___

January 18

| Dear God, today I am thankful for... | 20 ___ |

| Dear God, today I am thankful for... | 20 ___ |

| Dear God, today I am thankful for... | 20 ___ |

| Dear God, today I am thankful for... | 20 ___ |

| Dear God, today I am thankful for... | 20 ___ |

January 19

Dear God, today I am thankful for... | 20 ___

Dear God, today I am thankful for... | 20 ___

Dear God, today I am thankful for... | 20 ___

Dear God, today I am thankful for... | 20 ___

Dear God, today I am thankful for... | 20 ___

January 20

Dear God, today I am thankful for...   20 ____

. . . .

. . . .

. . . .

Dear God, today I am thankful for...   20 ____

. . . .

. . . .

. . . .

Dear God, today I am thankful for...   20 ____

. . . .

. . . .

. . . .

Dear God, today I am thankful for...   20 ____

. . . .

. . . .

. . . .

Dear God, today I am thankful for...   20 ____

. . . .

. . . .

. . . .

January 21

Dear God, today I am thankful for... | 20 ___

Dear God, today I am thankful for... | 20 ___

Dear God, today I am thankful for... | 20 ___

Dear God, today I am thankful for... | 20 ___

Dear God, today I am thankful for... | 20 ___

January 22

Dear God, today I am thankful for...   20 ___

....

....

....

....

Dear God, today I am thankful for...   20 ___

....

....

....

....

Dear God, today I am thankful for...   20 ___

....

....

....

....

Dear God, today I am thankful for...   20 ___

....

....

....

....

Dear God, today I am thankful for...   20 ___

....

....

....

....

January 23

Dear God, today I am thankful for... | 20 ___

Dear God, today I am thankful for... | 20 ___

Dear God, today I am thankful for... | 20 ___

Dear God, today I am thankful for... | 20 ___

Dear God, today I am thankful for... | 20 ___

January 24

Dear God, today I am thankful for... | 20 ___

Dear God, today I am thankful for... | 20 ___

Dear God, today I am thankful for... | 20 ___

Dear God, today I am thankful for... | 20 ___

Dear God, today I am thankful for... | 20 ___

January 25

Dear God, today I am thankful for... | 20 ___

Dear God, today I am thankful for... | 20 ___

Dear God, today I am thankful for... | 20 ___

Dear God, today I am thankful for... | 20 ___

Dear God, today I am thankful for... | 20 ___

January 26

Dear God, today I am thankful for... | 20 ___

Dear God, today I am thankful for... | 20 ___

Dear God, today I am thankful for... | 20 ___

Dear God, today I am thankful for... | 20 ___

Dear God, today I am thankful for... | 20 ___

January 27

| Dear God, today I am thankful for… | 20 ___ |

| Dear God, today I am thankful for… | 20 ___ |

| Dear God, today I am thankful for… | 20 ___ |

| Dear God, today I am thankful for… | 20 ___ |

| Dear God, today I am thankful for… | 20 ___ |

January 28

Dear God, today I am thankful for... | 20 ___

Dear God, today I am thankful for... | 20 ___

Dear God, today I am thankful for... | 20 ___

Dear God, today I am thankful for... | 20 ___

Dear God, today I am thankful for... | 20 ___

January 29

Dear God, today I am thankful for...	20 ___

Dear God, today I am thankful for...	20 ___

Dear God, today I am thankful for...	20 ___

Dear God, today I am thankful for...	20 ___

Dear God, today I am thankful for...	20 ___

January 30

Dear God, today I am thankful for...	20 ___

Dear God, today I am thankful for...	20 ___

Dear God, today I am thankful for...	20 ___

Dear God, today I am thankful for...	20 ___

Dear God, today I am thankful for...	20 ___

January 31

Dear God, today I am thankful for... | 20 ___

Dear God, today I am thankful for... | 20 ___

Dear God, today I am thankful for... | 20 ___

Dear God, today I am thankful for... | 20 ___

Dear God, today I am thankful for... | 20 ___

February 1

Dear God, today I am thankful for...	20 ___

Dear God, today I am thankful for...	20 ___

Dear God, today I am thankful for...	20 ___

Dear God, today I am thankful for...	20 ___

Dear God, today I am thankful for...	20 ___

February 2

Dear God, today I am thankful for...	20 ___

Dear God, today I am thankful for...	20 ___

Dear God, today I am thankful for...	20 ___

Dear God, today I am thankful for...	20 ___

Dear God, today I am thankful for...	20 ___

February 3

Dear God, today I am thankful for... | 20 ___

Dear God, today I am thankful for... | 20 ___

Dear God, today I am thankful for... | 20 ___

Dear God, today I am thankful for... | 20 ___

Dear God, today I am thankful for... | 20 ___

February 4

Dear God, today I am thankful for...   20 ___

Dear God, today I am thankful for...   20 ___

Dear God, today I am thankful for...   20 ___

Dear God, today I am thankful for...   20 ___

Dear God, today I am thankful for...   20 ___

February 5

| Dear God, today I am thankful for... | 20 ___ |

| Dear God, today I am thankful for... | 20 ___ |

| Dear God, today I am thankful for... | 20 ___ |

| Dear God, today I am thankful for... | 20 ___ |

| Dear God, today I am thankful for... | 20 ___ |

February 6

Dear God, today I am thankful for... | 20 ___

Dear God, today I am thankful for... | 20 ___

Dear God, today I am thankful for... | 20 ___

Dear God, today I am thankful for... | 20 ___

Dear God, today I am thankful for... | 20 ___

February 7

Dear God, today I am thankful for... | 20 ___

Dear God, today I am thankful for... | 20 ___

Dear God, today I am thankful for... | 20 ___

Dear God, today I am thankful for... | 20 ___

Dear God, today I am thankful for... | 20 ___

February 8

Dear God, today I am thankful for... | 20 ___

Dear God, today I am thankful for... | 20 ___

Dear God, today I am thankful for... | 20 ___

Dear God, today I am thankful for... | 20 ___

Dear God, today I am thankful for... | 20 ___

February 9

Dear God, today I am thankful for…   20 ___

Dear God, today I am thankful for…   20 ___

Dear God, today I am thankful for…   20 ___

Dear God, today I am thankful for…   20 ___

Dear God, today I am thankful for…   20 ___

February 10

Dear God, today I am thankful for...	20 ___

Dear God, today I am thankful for...	20 ___

Dear God, today I am thankful for...	20 ___

Dear God, today I am thankful for...	20 ___

Dear God, today I am thankful for...	20 ___

February 11

| Dear God, today I am thankful for... | 20 ___ |

| Dear God, today I am thankful for... | 20 ___ |

| Dear God, today I am thankful for... | 20 ___ |

| Dear God, today I am thankful for... | 20 ___ |

| Dear God, today I am thankful for... | 20 ___ |

February 12

Dear God, today I am thankful for...	20 ___

Dear God, today I am thankful for...	20 ___

Dear God, today I am thankful for...	20 ___

Dear God, today I am thankful for...	20 ___

Dear God, today I am thankful for...	20 ___

February 13

| Dear God, today I am thankful for... | 20 ___ |

| Dear God, today I am thankful for... | 20 ___ |

| Dear God, today I am thankful for... | 20 ___ |

| Dear God, today I am thankful for... | 20 ___ |

| Dear God, today I am thankful for... | 20 ___ |

February 14

| Dear God, today I am thankful for... | 20 ___ |

....
....
....

| Dear God, today I am thankful for... | 20 ___ |

....
....
....

| Dear God, today I am thankful for... | 20 ___ |

....
....
....

| Dear God, today I am thankful for... | 20 ___ |

....
....
....

| Dear God, today I am thankful for... | 20 ___ |

....
....
....

February 15

Dear God, today I am thankful for...   20 ___

Dear God, today I am thankful for...   20 ___

Dear God, today I am thankful for...   20 ___

Dear God, today I am thankful for...   20 ___

Dear God, today I am thankful for...   20 ___

February 16

| Dear God, today I am thankful for... | 20 ___ |

| Dear God, today I am thankful for... | 20 ___ |

| Dear God, today I am thankful for... | 20 ___ |

| Dear God, today I am thankful for... | 20 ___ |

| Dear God, today I am thankful for... | 20 ___ |

February 17

Dear God, today I am thankful for... | 20 ___

Dear God, today I am thankful for... | 20 ___

Dear God, today I am thankful for... | 20 ___

Dear God, today I am thankful for... | 20 ___

Dear God, today I am thankful for... | 20 ___

February 18

| Dear God, today I am thankful for… | 20 ___ |

| Dear God, today I am thankful for… | 20 ___ |

| Dear God, today I am thankful for… | 20 ___ |

| Dear God, today I am thankful for… | 20 ___ |

| Dear God, today I am thankful for… | 20 ___ |

February 19

Dear God, today I am thankful for... | 20 ___

Dear God, today I am thankful for... | 20 ___

Dear God, today I am thankful for... | 20 ___

Dear God, today I am thankful for... | 20 ___

Dear God, today I am thankful for... | 20 ___

February 20

Dear God, today I am thankful for...	*20 ___*

Dear God, today I am thankful for...	*20 ___*

Dear God, today I am thankful for...	*20 ___*

Dear God, today I am thankful for...	*20 ___*

Dear God, today I am thankful for...	*20 ___*

February 21

Dear God, today I am thankful for... | 20 ___

Dear God, today I am thankful for... | 20 ___

Dear God, today I am thankful for... | 20 ___

Dear God, today I am thankful for... | 20 ___

Dear God, today I am thankful for... | 20 ___

February 22

Dear God, today I am thankful for... | 20 ___

Dear God, today I am thankful for... | 20 ___

Dear God, today I am thankful for... | 20 ___

Dear God, today I am thankful for... | 20 ___

Dear God, today I am thankful for... | 20 ___

February 23

| Dear God, today I am thankful for... | 20 ___ |

....
....
....
....

| Dear God, today I am thankful for... | 20 ___ |

....
....
....
....

| Dear God, today I am thankful for... | 20 ___ |

....
....
....
....

| Dear God, today I am thankful for... | 20 ___ |

....
....
....
....

| Dear God, today I am thankful for... | 20 ___ |

....
....
....
....

February 24

| Dear God, today I am thankful for… | 20 ___ |

| Dear God, today I am thankful for… | 20 ___ |

| Dear God, today I am thankful for… | 20 ___ |

| Dear God, today I am thankful for… | 20 ___ |

| Dear God, today I am thankful for… | 20 ___ |

February 25

Dear God, today I am thankful for... | 20 ___

Dear God, today I am thankful for... | 20 ___

Dear God, today I am thankful for... | 20 ___

Dear God, today I am thankful for... | 20 ___

Dear God, today I am thankful for... | 20 ___

February 26

Dear God, today I am thankful for...	20 ___

Dear God, today I am thankful for...	20 ___

Dear God, today I am thankful for...	20 ___

Dear God, today I am thankful for...	20 ___

Dear God, today I am thankful for...	20 ___

February 27

Dear God, today I am thankful for... | 20 ___

Dear God, today I am thankful for... | 20 ___

Dear God, today I am thankful for... | 20 ___

Dear God, today I am thankful for... | 20 ___

Dear God, today I am thankful for... | 20 ___

February 28

Dear God, today I am thankful for... | 20 ___

Dear God, today I am thankful for... | 20 ___

Dear God, today I am thankful for... | 20 ___

Dear God, today I am thankful for... | 20 ___

Dear God, today I am thankful for... | 20 ___

February 29

| Dear God, today I am thankful for... | 20 ___ |

| Dear God, today I am thankful for... | 20 ___ |

| Dear God, today I am thankful for... | 20 ___ |

| Dear God, today I am thankful for... | 20 ___ |

| Dear God, today I am thankful for... | 20 ___ |

March 1

Dear God, today I am thankful for... | 20 ___

Dear God, today I am thankful for... | 20 ___

Dear God, today I am thankful for... | 20 ___

Dear God, today I am thankful for... | 20 ___

Dear God, today I am thankful for... | 20 ___

March 2

Dear God, today I am thankful for... | 20 ___
....
....
....
....

Dear God, today I am thankful for... | 20 ___
....
....
....
....

Dear God, today I am thankful for... | 20 ___
....
....
....
....

Dear God, today I am thankful for... | 20 ___
....
....
....
....

Dear God, today I am thankful for... | 20 ___
....
....
....
....

March 3

Dear God, today I am thankful for... | 20 ___

Dear God, today I am thankful for... | 20 ___

Dear God, today I am thankful for... | 20 ___

Dear God, today I am thankful for... | 20 ___

Dear God, today I am thankful for... | 20 ___

March 4

Dear God, today I am thankful for... | 20 ___

Dear God, today I am thankful for... | 20 ___

Dear God, today I am thankful for... | 20 ___

Dear God, today I am thankful for... | 20 ___

Dear God, today I am thankful for... | 20 ___

March 5

Dear God, today I am thankful for... | 20 ___

Dear God, today I am thankful for... | 20 ___

Dear God, today I am thankful for... | 20 ___

Dear God, today I am thankful for... | 20 ___

Dear God, today I am thankful for... | 20 ___

March 6

Dear God, today I am thankful for...	20 ___

Dear God, today I am thankful for...	20 ___

Dear God, today I am thankful for...	20 ___

Dear God, today I am thankful for...	20 ___

Dear God, today I am thankful for...	20 ___

March 7

Dear God, today I am thankful for... | 20 ___

Dear God, today I am thankful for... | 20 ___

Dear God, today I am thankful for... | 20 ___

Dear God, today I am thankful for... | 20 ___

Dear God, today I am thankful for... | 20 ___

March 8

Dear God, today I am thankful for...	20 ___

Dear God, today I am thankful for...	20 ___

Dear God, today I am thankful for...	20 ___

Dear God, today I am thankful for...	20 ___

Dear God, today I am thankful for...	20 ___

March 9

Dear God, today I am thankful for... | 20 ___

Dear God, today I am thankful for... | 20 ___

Dear God, today I am thankful for... | 20 ___

Dear God, today I am thankful for... | 20 ___

Dear God, today I am thankful for... | 20 ___

March 10

| Dear God, today I am thankful for... | 20 ___ |

....

....

....

....

| Dear God, today I am thankful for... | 20 ___ |

....

....

....

....

| Dear God, today I am thankful for... | 20 ___ |

....

....

....

....

| Dear God, today I am thankful for... | 20 ___ |

....

....

....

....

| Dear God, today I am thankful for... | 20 ___ |

....

....

....

....

March 11

Dear God, today I am thankful for...   20 ___

Dear God, today I am thankful for...   20 ___

Dear God, today I am thankful for...   20 ___

Dear God, today I am thankful for...   20 ___

Dear God, today I am thankful for...   20 ___

March 12

Dear God, today I am thankful for... | 20 ___

Dear God, today I am thankful for... | 20 ___

Dear God, today I am thankful for... | 20 ___

Dear God, today I am thankful for... | 20 ___

Dear God, today I am thankful for... | 20 ___

March 13

Dear God, today I am thankful for... | 20 ___

....
....
....
....

Dear God, today I am thankful for... | 20 ___

....
....
....
....

Dear God, today I am thankful for... | 20 ___

....
....
....
....

Dear God, today I am thankful for... | 20 ___

....
....
....
....

Dear God, today I am thankful for... | 20 ___

....
....
....
....

March 14

Dear God, today I am thankful for... | 20 ___

Dear God, today I am thankful for... | 20 ___

Dear God, today I am thankful for... | 20 ___

Dear God, today I am thankful for... | 20 ___

Dear God, today I am thankful for... | 20 ___

March 15

Dear God, today I am thankful for...   20 ___

Dear God, today I am thankful for...   20 ___

Dear God, today I am thankful for...   20 ___

Dear God, today I am thankful for...   20 ___

Dear God, today I am thankful for...   20 ___

March 16

Dear God, today I am thankful for... | 20 ___

Dear God, today I am thankful for... | 20 ___

Dear God, today I am thankful for... | 20 ___

Dear God, today I am thankful for... | 20 ___

Dear God, today I am thankful for... | 20 ___

March 17

Dear God, today I am thankful for... | 20 ___

Dear God, today I am thankful for... | 20 ___

Dear God, today I am thankful for... | 20 ___

Dear God, today I am thankful for... | 20 ___

Dear God, today I am thankful for... | 20 ___

March 18

Dear God, today I am thankful for... | 20 ___

Dear God, today I am thankful for... | 20 ___

Dear God, today I am thankful for... | 20 ___

Dear God, today I am thankful for... | 20 ___

Dear God, today I am thankful for... | 20 ___

March 19

Dear God, today I am thankful for...	20 ___

Dear God, today I am thankful for...	20 ___

Dear God, today I am thankful for...	20 ___

Dear God, today I am thankful for...	20 ___

Dear God, today I am thankful for...	20 ___

March 20

Dear God, today I am thankful for…	20 ___

Dear God, today I am thankful for…	20 ___

Dear God, today I am thankful for…	20 ___

Dear God, today I am thankful for…	20 ___

Dear God, today I am thankful for…	20 ___

March 21

Dear God, today I am thankful for...	20 ___

Dear God, today I am thankful for...	20 ___

Dear God, today I am thankful for...	20 ___

Dear God, today I am thankful for...	20 ___

Dear God, today I am thankful for...	20 ___

March 22

Dear God, today I am thankful for... | 20 ___

Dear God, today I am thankful for... | 20 ___

Dear God, today I am thankful for... | 20 ___

Dear God, today I am thankful for... | 20 ___

Dear God, today I am thankful for... | 20 ___

March 23

Dear God, today I am thankful for... | 20 ___

Dear God, today I am thankful for... | 20 ___

Dear God, today I am thankful for... | 20 ___

Dear God, today I am thankful for... | 20 ___

Dear God, today I am thankful for... | 20 ___

March 24

Dear God, today I am thankful for... | 20 ___

....
....
....
....

Dear God, today I am thankful for... | 20 ___

....
....
....
....

Dear God, today I am thankful for... | 20 ___

....
....
....
....

Dear God, today I am thankful for... | 20 ___

....
....
....
....

Dear God, today I am thankful for... | 20 ___

....
....
....
....

March 25

Dear God, today I am thankful for...   20 ___

....
....
....

Dear God, today I am thankful for...   20 ___

....
....
....

Dear God, today I am thankful for...   20 ___

....
....
....

Dear God, today I am thankful for...   20 ___

....
....
....

Dear God, today I am thankful for...   20 ___

....
....
....

March 26

Dear God, today I am thankful for... 20 ___

....
....
....
....

Dear God, today I am thankful for... 20 ___

....
....
....
....

Dear God, today I am thankful for... 20 ___

....
....
....
....

Dear God, today I am thankful for... 20 ___

....
....
....
....

Dear God, today I am thankful for... 20 ___

....
....
....
....

March 27

Dear God, today I am thankful for... | 20 ___

Dear God, today I am thankful for... | 20 ___

Dear God, today I am thankful for... | 20 ___

Dear God, today I am thankful for... | 20 ___

Dear God, today I am thankful for... | 20 ___

March 28

Dear God, today I am thankful for... | 20 ___

Dear God, today I am thankful for... | 20 ___

Dear God, today I am thankful for... | 20 ___

Dear God, today I am thankful for... | 20 ___

Dear God, today I am thankful for... | 20 ___

March 29

| Dear God, today I am thankful for… | 20 ___ |

| Dear God, today I am thankful for… | 20 ___ |

| Dear God, today I am thankful for… | 20 ___ |

| Dear God, today I am thankful for… | 20 ___ |

| Dear God, today I am thankful for… | 20 ___ |

March 30

| Dear God, today I am thankful for... | 20 ___ |

| Dear God, today I am thankful for... | 20 ___ |

| Dear God, today I am thankful for... | 20 ___ |

| Dear God, today I am thankful for... | 20 ___ |

| Dear God, today I am thankful for... | 20 ___ |

March 31

Dear God, today I am thankful for...	20 ___

Dear God, today I am thankful for...	20 ___

Dear God, today I am thankful for...	20 ___

Dear God, today I am thankful for...	20 ___

Dear God, today I am thankful for...	20 ___

April 1

Dear God, today I am thankful for... | 20 ___

Dear God, today I am thankful for... | 20 ___

Dear God, today I am thankful for... | 20 ___

Dear God, today I am thankful for... | 20 ___

Dear God, today I am thankful for... | 20 ___

April 2

Dear God, today I am thankful for...	20 ___

Dear God, today I am thankful for...	20 ___

Dear God, today I am thankful for...	20 ___

Dear God, today I am thankful for...	20 ___

Dear God, today I am thankful for...	20 ___

April 3

Dear God, today I am thankful for... | 20 ___

Dear God, today I am thankful for... | 20 ___

Dear God, today I am thankful for... | 20 ___

Dear God, today I am thankful for... | 20 ___

Dear God, today I am thankful for... | 20 ___

April 4

| Dear God, today I am thankful for... | 20 ___ |

....
....
....
....

| Dear God, today I am thankful for... | 20 ___ |

....
....
....
....

| Dear God, today I am thankful for... | 20 ___ |

....
....
....
....

| Dear God, today I am thankful for... | 20 ___ |

....
....
....
....

| Dear God, today I am thankful for... | 20 ___ |

....
....
....
....

April 5

Dear God, today I am thankful for... | 20 ___

Dear God, today I am thankful for... | 20 ___

Dear God, today I am thankful for... | 20 ___

Dear God, today I am thankful for... | 20 ___

Dear God, today I am thankful for... | 20 ___

April 6

Dear God, today I am thankful for… 20 ___

Dear God, today I am thankful for… 20 ___

Dear God, today I am thankful for… 20 ___

Dear God, today I am thankful for… 20 ___

Dear God, today I am thankful for… 20 ___

April 7

Dear God, today I am thankful for...	20 ___

Dear God, today I am thankful for...	20 ___

Dear God, today I am thankful for...	20 ___

Dear God, today I am thankful for...	20 ___

Dear God, today I am thankful for...	20 ___

April 8

Dear God, today I am thankful for... | 20 ___

Dear God, today I am thankful for... | 20 ___

Dear God, today I am thankful for... | 20 ___

Dear God, today I am thankful for... | 20 ___

Dear God, today I am thankful for... | 20 ___

April 9

Dear God, today I am thankful for... | 20 ___

Dear God, today I am thankful for... | 20 ___

Dear God, today I am thankful for... | 20 ___

Dear God, today I am thankful for... | 20 ___

Dear God, today I am thankful for... | 20 ___

April 10

Dear God, today I am thankful for...   20 ___

Dear God, today I am thankful for...   20 ___

Dear God, today I am thankful for...   20 ___

Dear God, today I am thankful for...   20 ___

Dear God, today I am thankful for...   20 ___

April 11

Dear God, today I am thankful for... | 20 ___

Dear God, today I am thankful for... | 20 ___

Dear God, today I am thankful for... | 20 ___

Dear God, today I am thankful for... | 20 ___

Dear God, today I am thankful for... | 20 ___

April 12

Dear God, today I am thankful for... | 20 ___

Dear God, today I am thankful for... | 20 ___

Dear God, today I am thankful for... | 20 ___

Dear God, today I am thankful for... | 20 ___

Dear God, today I am thankful for... | 20 ___

April 13

Dear God, today I am thankful for... | 20 ___

Dear God, today I am thankful for... | 20 ___

Dear God, today I am thankful for... | 20 ___

Dear God, today I am thankful for... | 20 ___

Dear God, today I am thankful for... | 20 ___

April 14

Dear God, today I am thankful for...	20 ___

Dear God, today I am thankful for...	20 ___

Dear God, today I am thankful for...	20 ___

Dear God, today I am thankful for...	20 ___

Dear God, today I am thankful for...	20 ___

April 15

Dear God, today I am thankful for... | 20 ___

Dear God, today I am thankful for... | 20 ___

Dear God, today I am thankful for... | 20 ___

Dear God, today I am thankful for... | 20 ___

Dear God, today I am thankful for... | 20 ___

April 16

Dear God, today I am thankful for...   20 ___

....
....
....
....

Dear God, today I am thankful for...   20 ___

....
....
....
....

Dear God, today I am thankful for...   20 ___

....
....
....
....

Dear God, today I am thankful for...   20 ___

....
....
....
....

Dear God, today I am thankful for...   20 ___

....
....
....
....

April 17

Dear God, today I am thankful for...	20 ___

Dear God, today I am thankful for...	20 ___

Dear God, today I am thankful for...	20 ___

Dear God, today I am thankful for...	20 ___

Dear God, today I am thankful for...	20 ___

April 18

| Dear God, today I am thankful for... | 20 ___ |

| Dear God, today I am thankful for... | 20 ___ |

| Dear God, today I am thankful for... | 20 ___ |

| Dear God, today I am thankful for... | 20 ___ |

| Dear God, today I am thankful for... | 20 ___ |

April 19

Dear God, today I am thankful for... | 20 ___

Dear God, today I am thankful for... | 20 ___

Dear God, today I am thankful for... | 20 ___

Dear God, today I am thankful for... | 20 ___

Dear God, today I am thankful for... | 20 ___

April 20

| Dear God, today I am thankful for... | 20 ___ |

| Dear God, today I am thankful for... | 20 ___ |

| Dear God, today I am thankful for... | 20 ___ |

| Dear God, today I am thankful for... | 20 ___ |

| Dear God, today I am thankful for... | 20 ___ |

April 21

Dear God, today I am thankful for... | 20 ___

Dear God, today I am thankful for... | 20 ___

Dear God, today I am thankful for... | 20 ___

Dear God, today I am thankful for... | 20 ___

Dear God, today I am thankful for... | 20 ___

April 22

Dear God, today I am thankful for... | 20 ___

Dear God, today I am thankful for... | 20 ___

Dear God, today I am thankful for... | 20 ___

Dear God, today I am thankful for... | 20 ___

Dear God, today I am thankful for... | 20 ___

April 23

Dear God, today I am thankful for... | 20 ___

....
....
....
....

Dear God, today I am thankful for... | 20 ___

....
....
....
....

Dear God, today I am thankful for... | 20 ___

....
....
....
....

Dear God, today I am thankful for... | 20 ___

....
....
....
....

Dear God, today I am thankful for... | 20 ___

....
....
....
....

April 24

Dear God, today I am thankful for... | 20 ___

Dear God, today I am thankful for... | 20 ___

Dear God, today I am thankful for... | 20 ___

Dear God, today I am thankful for... | 20 ___

Dear God, today I am thankful for... | 20 ___

April 25

Dear God, today I am thankful for... | 20 ___

Dear God, today I am thankful for... | 20 ___

Dear God, today I am thankful for... | 20 ___

Dear God, today I am thankful for... | 20 ___

Dear God, today I am thankful for... | 20 ___

April 26

Dear God, today I am thankful for... | 20 ___

Dear God, today I am thankful for... | 20 ___

Dear God, today I am thankful for... | 20 ___

Dear God, today I am thankful for... | 20 ___

Dear God, today I am thankful for... | 20 ___

April 27

Dear God, today I am thankful for... | 20 ___

Dear God, today I am thankful for... | 20 ___

Dear God, today I am thankful for... | 20 ___

Dear God, today I am thankful for... | 20 ___

Dear God, today I am thankful for... | 20 ___

April 28

Dear God, today I am thankful for...	20 ___

Dear God, today I am thankful for...	20 ___

Dear God, today I am thankful for...	20 ___

Dear God, today I am thankful for...	20 ___

Dear God, today I am thankful for...	20 ___

April 29

Dear God, today I am thankful for... | 20 ___

Dear God, today I am thankful for... | 20 ___

Dear God, today I am thankful for... | 20 ___

Dear God, today I am thankful for... | 20 ___

Dear God, today I am thankful for... | 20 ___

April 30

Dear God, today I am thankful for...   20 ___

Dear God, today I am thankful for...   20 ___

Dear God, today I am thankful for...   20 ___

Dear God, today I am thankful for...   20 ___

Dear God, today I am thankful for...   20 ___

May 1

Dear God, today I am thankful for... | 20 ___

Dear God, today I am thankful for... | 20 ___

Dear God, today I am thankful for... | 20 ___

Dear God, today I am thankful for... | 20 ___

Dear God, today I am thankful for... | 20 ___

May 2

Dear God, today I am thankful for... | 20 ___

Dear God, today I am thankful for... | 20 ___

Dear God, today I am thankful for... | 20 ___

Dear God, today I am thankful for... | 20 ___

Dear God, today I am thankful for... | 20 ___

May 3

Dear God, today I am thankful for...	20 ___

Dear God, today I am thankful for...	20 ___

Dear God, today I am thankful for...	20 ___

Dear God, today I am thankful for...	20 ___

Dear God, today I am thankful for...	20 ___

May 4

| *Dear God, today I am thankful for…* | 20 ___ |

| *Dear God, today I am thankful for…* | 20 ___ |

| *Dear God, today I am thankful for…* | 20 ___ |

| *Dear God, today I am thankful for…* | 20 ___ |

| *Dear God, today I am thankful for…* | 20 ___ |

May 5

Dear God, today I am thankful for... | 20 ___

Dear God, today I am thankful for... | 20 ___

Dear God, today I am thankful for... | 20 ___

Dear God, today I am thankful for... | 20 ___

Dear God, today I am thankful for... | 20 ___

May 6

Dear God, today I am thankful for... | 20 ___

Dear God, today I am thankful for... | 20 ___

Dear God, today I am thankful for... | 20 ___

Dear God, today I am thankful for... | 20 ___

Dear God, today I am thankful for... | 20 ___

May 7

Dear God, today I am thankful for... | 20 ___

Dear God, today I am thankful for... | 20 ___

Dear God, today I am thankful for... | 20 ___

Dear God, today I am thankful for... | 20 ___

Dear God, today I am thankful for... | 20 ___

May 8

Dear God, today I am thankful for... | 20 ___

Dear God, today I am thankful for... | 20 ___

Dear God, today I am thankful for... | 20 ___

Dear God, today I am thankful for... | 20 ___

Dear God, today I am thankful for... | 20 ___

May 9

Dear God, today I am thankful for... | 20 ___

Dear God, today I am thankful for... | 20 ___

Dear God, today I am thankful for... | 20 ___

Dear God, today I am thankful for... | 20 ___

Dear God, today I am thankful for... | 20 ___

May 10

Dear God, today I am thankful for...	20 ___

Dear God, today I am thankful for...	20 ___

Dear God, today I am thankful for...	20 ___

Dear God, today I am thankful for...	20 ___

Dear God, today I am thankful for...	20 ___

May 11

Dear God, today I am thankful for... | 20 ___

Dear God, today I am thankful for... | 20 ___

Dear God, today I am thankful for... | 20 ___

Dear God, today I am thankful for... | 20 ___

Dear God, today I am thankful for... | 20 ___

May 12

| Dear God, today I am thankful for... | 20 ___ |

| Dear God, today I am thankful for... | 20 ___ |

| Dear God, today I am thankful for... | 20 ___ |

| Dear God, today I am thankful for... | 20 ___ |

| Dear God, today I am thankful for... | 20 ___ |

May 13

Dear God, today I am thankful for... | 20 ___

Dear God, today I am thankful for... | 20 ___

Dear God, today I am thankful for... | 20 ___

Dear God, today I am thankful for... | 20 ___

Dear God, today I am thankful for... | 20 ___

May 14

Dear God, today I am thankful for... | 20 ___

Dear God, today I am thankful for... | 20 ___

Dear God, today I am thankful for... | 20 ___

Dear God, today I am thankful for... | 20 ___

Dear God, today I am thankful for... | 20 ___

May 15

Dear God, today I am thankful for... | 20 ___

Dear God, today I am thankful for... | 20 ___

Dear God, today I am thankful for... | 20 ___

Dear God, today I am thankful for... | 20 ___

Dear God, today I am thankful for... | 20 ___

May 16

Dear God, today I am thankful for... | 20 ___

Dear God, today I am thankful for... | 20 ___

Dear God, today I am thankful for... | 20 ___

Dear God, today I am thankful for... | 20 ___

Dear God, today I am thankful for... | 20 ___

May 17

Dear God, today I am thankful for... | 20 ___

Dear God, today I am thankful for... | 20 ___

Dear God, today I am thankful for... | 20 ___

Dear God, today I am thankful for... | 20 ___

Dear God, today I am thankful for... | 20 ___

May 18

Dear God, today I am thankful for... | 20 ___

Dear God, today I am thankful for... | 20 ___

Dear God, today I am thankful for... | 20 ___

Dear God, today I am thankful for... | 20 ___

Dear God, today I am thankful for... | 20 ___

May 19

Dear God, today I am thankful for... | 20 ___

....
....
....
....

Dear God, today I am thankful for... | 20 ___

....
....
....
....

Dear God, today I am thankful for... | 20 ___

....
....
....
....

Dear God, today I am thankful for... | 20 ___

....
....
....
....

Dear God, today I am thankful for... | 20 ___

....
....
....
....

May 20

Dear God, today I am thankful for... | 20 ___

Dear God, today I am thankful for... | 20 ___

Dear God, today I am thankful for... | 20 ___

Dear God, today I am thankful for... | 20 ___

Dear God, today I am thankful for... | 20 ___

May 21

Dear God, today I am thankful for...	20 ___

Dear God, today I am thankful for...	20 ___

Dear God, today I am thankful for...	20 ___

Dear God, today I am thankful for...	20 ___

Dear God, today I am thankful for...	20 ___

May 22

| Dear God, today I am thankful for... | 20 ___ |

| Dear God, today I am thankful for... | 20 ___ |

| Dear God, today I am thankful for... | 20 ___ |

| Dear God, today I am thankful for... | 20 ___ |

| Dear God, today I am thankful for... | 20 ___ |

May 23

Dear God, today I am thankful for... | 20 ___

Dear God, today I am thankful for... | 20 ___

Dear God, today I am thankful for... | 20 ___

Dear God, today I am thankful for... | 20 ___

Dear God, today I am thankful for... | 20 ___

May 24

Dear God, today I am thankful for... | 20 ___

Dear God, today I am thankful for... | 20 ___

Dear God, today I am thankful for... | 20 ___

Dear God, today I am thankful for... | 20 ___

Dear God, today I am thankful for... | 20 ___

May 25

Dear God, today I am thankful for... | 20 ___

Dear God, today I am thankful for... | 20 ___

Dear God, today I am thankful for... | 20 ___

Dear God, today I am thankful for... | 20 ___

Dear God, today I am thankful for... | 20 ___

May 26

Dear God, today I am thankful for... | 20 ___

Dear God, today I am thankful for... | 20 ___

Dear God, today I am thankful for... | 20 ___

Dear God, today I am thankful for... | 20 ___

Dear God, today I am thankful for... | 20 ___

May 27

Dear God, today I am thankful for...	20 ___

Dear God, today I am thankful for...	20 ___

Dear God, today I am thankful for...	20 ___

Dear God, today I am thankful for...	20 ___

Dear God, today I am thankful for...	20 ___

May 28

Dear God, today I am thankful for...	*20* ___

Dear God, today I am thankful for...	*20* ___

Dear God, today I am thankful for...	*20* ___

Dear God, today I am thankful for...	*20* ___

Dear God, today I am thankful for...	*20* ___

May 29

Dear God, today I am thankful for... | 20 ___

....

Dear God, today I am thankful for... | 20 ___

....

Dear God, today I am thankful for... | 20 ___

....

Dear God, today I am thankful for... | 20 ___

....

Dear God, today I am thankful for... | 20 ___

....

May 30

Dear God, today I am thankful for...	20 ___

Dear God, today I am thankful for...	20 ___

Dear God, today I am thankful for...	20 ___

Dear God, today I am thankful for...	20 ___

Dear God, today I am thankful for...	20 ___

May 31

Dear God, today I am thankful for... | 20 ___

Dear God, today I am thankful for... | 20 ___

Dear God, today I am thankful for... | 20 ___

Dear God, today I am thankful for... | 20 ___

Dear God, today I am thankful for... | 20 ___

June 1

Dear God, today I am thankful for... | 20 ____

Dear God, today I am thankful for... | 20 ____

Dear God, today I am thankful for... | 20 ____

Dear God, today I am thankful for... | 20 ____

Dear God, today I am thankful for... | 20 ____

June 2

Dear God, today I am thankful for...	20 ___

Dear God, today I am thankful for...	20 ___

Dear God, today I am thankful for...	20 ___

Dear God, today I am thankful for...	20 ___

Dear God, today I am thankful for...	20 ___

June 3

Dear God, today I am thankful for... | 20 ___

Dear God, today I am thankful for... | 20 ___

Dear God, today I am thankful for... | 20 ___

Dear God, today I am thankful for... | 20 ___

Dear God, today I am thankful for... | 20 ___

June 4

| Dear God, today I am thankful for... | 20 ___ |

| Dear God, today I am thankful for... | 20 ___ |

| Dear God, today I am thankful for... | 20 ___ |

| Dear God, today I am thankful for... | 20 ___ |

| Dear God, today I am thankful for... | 20 ___ |

June 5

Dear God, today I am thankful for… 20 ___

Dear God, today I am thankful for… 20 ___

Dear God, today I am thankful for… 20 ___

Dear God, today I am thankful for… 20 ___

Dear God, today I am thankful for… 20 ___

June 6

Dear God, today I am thankful for...	20 ___

Dear God, today I am thankful for...	20 ___

Dear God, today I am thankful for...	20 ___

Dear God, today I am thankful for...	20 ___

Dear God, today I am thankful for...	20 ___

June 7

Dear God, today I am thankful for...	20 ___

Dear God, today I am thankful for...	20 ___

Dear God, today I am thankful for...	20 ___

Dear God, today I am thankful for...	20 ___

Dear God, today I am thankful for...	20 ___

June 8

Dear God, today I am thankful for... | 20 ___

Dear God, today I am thankful for... | 20 ___

Dear God, today I am thankful for... | 20 ___

Dear God, today I am thankful for... | 20 ___

Dear God, today I am thankful for... | 20 ___

June 9

Dear God, today I am thankful for...	20 ___

Dear God, today I am thankful for...	20 ___

Dear God, today I am thankful for...	20 ___

Dear God, today I am thankful for...	20 ___

Dear God, today I am thankful for...	20 ___

June 10

Dear God, today I am thankful for...	20 ___

Dear God, today I am thankful for...	20 ___

Dear God, today I am thankful for...	20 ___

Dear God, today I am thankful for...	20 ___

Dear God, today I am thankful for...	20 ___

June 11

Dear God, today I am thankful for... | 20 ___

Dear God, today I am thankful for... | 20 ___

Dear God, today I am thankful for... | 20 ___

Dear God, today I am thankful for... | 20 ___

Dear God, today I am thankful for... | 20 ___

June 12

| Dear God, today I am thankful for... | 20 ___ |

| Dear God, today I am thankful for... | 20 ___ |

| Dear God, today I am thankful for... | 20 ___ |

| Dear God, today I am thankful for... | 20 ___ |

| Dear God, today I am thankful for... | 20 ___ |

June 13

Dear God, today I am thankful for... | 20 ___

Dear God, today I am thankful for... | 20 ___

Dear God, today I am thankful for... | 20 ___

Dear God, today I am thankful for... | 20 ___

Dear God, today I am thankful for... | 20 ___

June 14

Dear God, today I am thankful for...   20 ___

....
....
....
....

Dear God, today I am thankful for...   20 ___

....
....
....
....

Dear God, today I am thankful for...   20 ___

....
....
....
....

Dear God, today I am thankful for...   20 ___

....
....
....
....

Dear God, today I am thankful for...   20 ___

....
....
....
....

June 15

Dear God, today I am thankful for... | 20 ___

....
....
....
....

Dear God, today I am thankful for... | 20 ___

....
....
....
....

Dear God, today I am thankful for... | 20 ___

....
....
....
....

Dear God, today I am thankful for... | 20 ___

....
....
....
....

Dear God, today I am thankful for... | 20 ___

....
....
....
....

June 16

Dear God, today I am thankful for... | 20 ___

Dear God, today I am thankful for... | 20 ___

Dear God, today I am thankful for... | 20 ___

Dear God, today I am thankful for... | 20 ___

Dear God, today I am thankful for... | 20 ___

June 17

Dear God, today I am thankful for... | 20 ___

Dear God, today I am thankful for... | 20 ___

Dear God, today I am thankful for... | 20 ___

Dear God, today I am thankful for... | 20 ___

Dear God, today I am thankful for... | 20 ___

June 18

Dear God, today I am thankful for... | 20 ___

Dear God, today I am thankful for... | 20 ___

Dear God, today I am thankful for... | 20 ___

Dear God, today I am thankful for... | 20 ___

Dear God, today I am thankful for... | 20 ___

June 19

Dear God, today I am thankful for... | 20 ___

Dear God, today I am thankful for... | 20 ___

Dear God, today I am thankful for... | 20 ___

Dear God, today I am thankful for... | 20 ___

Dear God, today I am thankful for... | 20 ___

June 20

Dear God, today I am thankful for... | 20 ___

Dear God, today I am thankful for... | 20 ___

Dear God, today I am thankful for... | 20 ___

Dear God, today I am thankful for... | 20 ___

Dear God, today I am thankful for... | 20 ___

June 21

Dear God, today I am thankful for... | 20 ___

Dear God, today I am thankful for... | 20 ___

Dear God, today I am thankful for... | 20 ___

Dear God, today I am thankful for... | 20 ___

Dear God, today I am thankful for... | 20 ___

June 22

Dear God, today I am thankful for... | 20 ___

Dear God, today I am thankful for... | 20 ___

Dear God, today I am thankful for... | 20 ___

Dear God, today I am thankful for... | 20 ___

Dear God, today I am thankful for... | 20 ___

June 23

Dear God, today I am thankful for...	20 ___

Dear God, today I am thankful for...	20 ___

Dear God, today I am thankful for...	20 ___

Dear God, today I am thankful for...	20 ___

Dear God, today I am thankful for...	20 ___

June 24

Dear God, today I am thankful for... | 20 ___

Dear God, today I am thankful for... | 20 ___

Dear God, today I am thankful for... | 20 ___

Dear God, today I am thankful for... | 20 ___

Dear God, today I am thankful for... | 20 ___

June 25

Dear God, today I am thankful for...	20 ___

Dear God, today I am thankful for...	20 ___

Dear God, today I am thankful for...	20 ___

Dear God, today I am thankful for...	20 ___

Dear God, today I am thankful for...	20 ___

June 26

Dear God, today I am thankful for... | 20 ___

Dear God, today I am thankful for... | 20 ___

Dear God, today I am thankful for... | 20 ___

Dear God, today I am thankful for... | 20 ___

Dear God, today I am thankful for... | 20 ___

June 27

Dear God, today I am thankful for...	20 ___

Dear God, today I am thankful for...	20 ___

Dear God, today I am thankful for...	20 ___

Dear God, today I am thankful for...	20 ___

Dear God, today I am thankful for...	20 ___

June 28

Dear God, today I am thankful for... | 20 ___

Dear God, today I am thankful for... | 20 ___

Dear God, today I am thankful for... | 20 ___

Dear God, today I am thankful for... | 20 ___

Dear God, today I am thankful for... | 20 ___

June 29

Dear God, today I am thankful for... | 20 ___

Dear God, today I am thankful for... | 20 ___

Dear God, today I am thankful for... | 20 ___

Dear God, today I am thankful for... | 20 ___

Dear God, today I am thankful for... | 20 ___

June 30

Dear God, today I am thankful for... | 20 ___

Dear God, today I am thankful for... | 20 ___

Dear God, today I am thankful for... | 20 ___

Dear God, today I am thankful for... | 20 ___

Dear God, today I am thankful for... | 20 ___

July 1

Dear God, today I am thankful for...	20 ___

Dear God, today I am thankful for...	20 ___

Dear God, today I am thankful for...	20 ___

Dear God, today I am thankful for...	20 ___

Dear God, today I am thankful for...	20 ___

July 2

Dear God, today I am thankful for...   20 ___

Dear God, today I am thankful for...   20 ___

Dear God, today I am thankful for...   20 ___

Dear God, today I am thankful for...   20 ___

Dear God, today I am thankful for...   20 ___

July 3

Dear God, today I am thankful for... | 20 ___

Dear God, today I am thankful for... | 20 ___

Dear God, today I am thankful for... | 20 ___

Dear God, today I am thankful for... | 20 ___

Dear God, today I am thankful for... | 20 ___

July 4

Dear God, today I am thankful for... | 20 ___

Dear God, today I am thankful for... | 20 ___

Dear God, today I am thankful for... | 20 ___

Dear God, today I am thankful for... | 20 ___

Dear God, today I am thankful for... | 20 ___

July 5

Dear God, today I am thankful for...   20 ___

Dear God, today I am thankful for...   20 ___

Dear God, today I am thankful for...   20 ___

Dear God, today I am thankful for...   20 ___

Dear God, today I am thankful for...   20 ___

July 6

Dear God, today I am thankful for... | 20 ____

Dear God, today I am thankful for... | 20 ____

Dear God, today I am thankful for... | 20 ____

Dear God, today I am thankful for... | 20 ____

Dear God, today I am thankful for... | 20 ____

July 7

| Dear God, today I am thankful for… | 20 ___ |

| Dear God, today I am thankful for… | 20 ___ |

| Dear God, today I am thankful for… | 20 ___ |

| Dear God, today I am thankful for… | 20 ___ |

| Dear God, today I am thankful for… | 20 ___ |

July 8

Dear God, today I am thankful for... | 20 ___

Dear God, today I am thankful for... | 20 ___

Dear God, today I am thankful for... | 20 ___

Dear God, today I am thankful for... | 20 ___

Dear God, today I am thankful for... | 20 ___

July 9

Dear God, today I am thankful for... | 20 ___

Dear God, today I am thankful for... | 20 ___

Dear God, today I am thankful for... | 20 ___

Dear God, today I am thankful for... | 20 ___

Dear God, today I am thankful for... | 20 ___

July 10

Dear God, today I am thankful for... | 20 ___

Dear God, today I am thankful for... | 20 ___

Dear God, today I am thankful for... | 20 ___

Dear God, today I am thankful for... | 20 ___

Dear God, today I am thankful for... | 20 ___

July 11

Dear God, today I am thankful for... | 20 ___

Dear God, today I am thankful for... | 20 ___

Dear God, today I am thankful for... | 20 ___

Dear God, today I am thankful for... | 20 ___

Dear God, today I am thankful for... | 20 ___

July 12

Dear God, today I am thankful for... | 20 ___

Dear God, today I am thankful for... | 20 ___

Dear God, today I am thankful for... | 20 ___

Dear God, today I am thankful for... | 20 ___

Dear God, today I am thankful for... | 20 ___

July 13

Dear God, today I am thankful for... | 20 ___

Dear God, today I am thankful for... | 20 ___

Dear God, today I am thankful for... | 20 ___

Dear God, today I am thankful for... | 20 ___

Dear God, today I am thankful for... | 20 ___

July 14

Dear God, today I am thankful for... | 20 ___

Dear God, today I am thankful for... | 20 ___

Dear God, today I am thankful for... | 20 ___

Dear God, today I am thankful for... | 20 ___

Dear God, today I am thankful for... | 20 ___

July 15

Dear God, today I am thankful for... 20 ___

Dear God, today I am thankful for... 20 ___

Dear God, today I am thankful for... 20 ___

Dear God, today I am thankful for... 20 ___

Dear God, today I am thankful for... 20 ___

July 16

Dear God, today I am thankful for... | 20 ___

Dear God, today I am thankful for... | 20 ___

Dear God, today I am thankful for... | 20 ___

Dear God, today I am thankful for... | 20 ___

Dear God, today I am thankful for... | 20 ___

July 17

Dear God, today I am thankful for... | 20 ___

Dear God, today I am thankful for... | 20 ___

Dear God, today I am thankful for... | 20 ___

Dear God, today I am thankful for... | 20 ___

Dear God, today I am thankful for... | 20 ___

July 18

| Dear God, today I am thankful for... | 20 ___ |

. . . .
. . . .
. . . .

| Dear God, today I am thankful for... | 20 ___ |

. . . .
. . . .
. . . .

| Dear God, today I am thankful for... | 20 ___ |

. . . .
. . . .
. . . .

| Dear God, today I am thankful for... | 20 ___ |

. . . .
. . . .
. . . .

| Dear God, today I am thankful for... | 20 ___ |

. . . .
. . . .
. . . .

July 19

Dear God, today I am thankful for...   20 ___

Dear God, today I am thankful for...   20 ___

Dear God, today I am thankful for...   20 ___

Dear God, today I am thankful for...   20 ___

Dear God, today I am thankful for...   20 ___

July 20

| Dear God, today I am thankful for... | 20 ___ |

| Dear God, today I am thankful for... | 20 ___ |

| Dear God, today I am thankful for... | 20 ___ |

| Dear God, today I am thankful for... | 20 ___ |

| Dear God, today I am thankful for... | 20 ___ |

July 21

Dear God, today I am thankful for... | 20 ___

....
....
....
....

Dear God, today I am thankful for... | 20 ___

....
....
....
....

Dear God, today I am thankful for... | 20 ___

....
....
....
....

Dear God, today I am thankful for... | 20 ___

....
....
....
....

Dear God, today I am thankful for... | 20 ___

....
....
....
....

July 22

Dear God, today I am thankful for... | 20 ___

Dear God, today I am thankful for... | 20 ___

Dear God, today I am thankful for... | 20 ___

Dear God, today I am thankful for... | 20 ___

Dear God, today I am thankful for... | 20 ___

July 23

Dear God, today I am thankful for... | 20 ___

Dear God, today I am thankful for... | 20 ___

Dear God, today I am thankful for... | 20 ___

Dear God, today I am thankful for... | 20 ___

Dear God, today I am thankful for... | 20 ___

July 24

Dear God, today I am thankful for... | 20 ___

Dear God, today I am thankful for... | 20 ___

Dear God, today I am thankful for... | 20 ___

Dear God, today I am thankful for... | 20 ___

Dear God, today I am thankful for... | 20 ___

July 25

Dear God, today I am thankful for... | 20 ___

Dear God, today I am thankful for... | 20 ___

Dear God, today I am thankful for... | 20 ___

Dear God, today I am thankful for... | 20 ___

Dear God, today I am thankful for... | 20 ___

July 26

Dear God, today I am thankful for... | 20 ___

Dear God, today I am thankful for... | 20 ___

Dear God, today I am thankful for... | 20 ___

Dear God, today I am thankful for... | 20 ___

Dear God, today I am thankful for... | 20 ___

July 27

Dear God, today I am thankful for... | 20 ___

....
....
....
....

Dear God, today I am thankful for... | 20 ___

....
....
....
....

Dear God, today I am thankful for... | 20 ___

....
....
....
....

Dear God, today I am thankful for... | 20 ___

....
....
....
....

Dear God, today I am thankful for... | 20 ___

....
....
....
....

July 28

Dear God, today I am thankful for...	20 ___

Dear God, today I am thankful for...	20 ___

Dear God, today I am thankful for...	20 ___

Dear God, today I am thankful for...	20 ___

Dear God, today I am thankful for...	20 ___

July 29

Dear God, today I am thankful for... | 20 ___

Dear God, today I am thankful for... | 20 ___

Dear God, today I am thankful for... | 20 ___

Dear God, today I am thankful for... | 20 ___

Dear God, today I am thankful for... | 20 ___

July 30

Dear God, today I am thankful for...   20 ___

Dear God, today I am thankful for...   20 ___

Dear God, today I am thankful for...   20 ___

Dear God, today I am thankful for...   20 ___

Dear God, today I am thankful for...   20 ___

July 31

Dear God, today I am thankful for...   20 ___

Dear God, today I am thankful for...   20 ___

Dear God, today I am thankful for...   20 ___

Dear God, today I am thankful for...   20 ___

Dear God, today I am thankful for...   20 ___

August 1

Dear God, today I am thankful for... | 20 ___

Dear God, today I am thankful for... | 20 ___

Dear God, today I am thankful for... | 20 ___

Dear God, today I am thankful for... | 20 ___

Dear God, today I am thankful for... | 20 ___

August 2

Dear God, today I am thankful for... | 20 ___

Dear God, today I am thankful for... | 20 ___

Dear God, today I am thankful for... | 20 ___

Dear God, today I am thankful for... | 20 ___

Dear God, today I am thankful for... | 20 ___

August 3

Dear God, today I am thankful for... | 20 ___

Dear God, today I am thankful for... | 20 ___

Dear God, today I am thankful for... | 20 ___

Dear God, today I am thankful for... | 20 ___

Dear God, today I am thankful for... | 20 ___

August 4

Dear God, today I am thankful for...   20 ___

Dear God, today I am thankful for...   20 ___

Dear God, today I am thankful for...   20 ___

Dear God, today I am thankful for...   20 ___

Dear God, today I am thankful for...   20 ___

August 5

Dear God, today I am thankful for... 20 ___

Dear God, today I am thankful for... 20 ___

Dear God, today I am thankful for... 20 ___

Dear God, today I am thankful for... 20 ___

Dear God, today I am thankful for... 20 ___

August 6

| Dear God, today I am thankful for... | 20 ___ |

| Dear God, today I am thankful for... | 20 ___ |

| Dear God, today I am thankful for... | 20 ___ |

| Dear God, today I am thankful for... | 20 ___ |

| Dear God, today I am thankful for... | 20 ___ |

August 7

Dear God, today I am thankful for... | 20 ___

Dear God, today I am thankful for... | 20 ___

Dear God, today I am thankful for... | 20 ___

Dear God, today I am thankful for... | 20 ___

Dear God, today I am thankful for... | 20 ___

August 8

Dear God, today I am thankful for... | 20 ___

Dear God, today I am thankful for... | 20 ___

Dear God, today I am thankful for... | 20 ___

Dear God, today I am thankful for... | 20 ___

Dear God, today I am thankful for... | 20 ___

August 9

| Dear God, today I am thankful for... | 20 ___ |

....
....
....
....

| Dear God, today I am thankful for... | 20 ___ |

....
....
....
....

| Dear God, today I am thankful for... | 20 ___ |

....
....
....
....

| Dear God, today I am thankful for... | 20 ___ |

....
....
....
....

| Dear God, today I am thankful for... | 20 ___ |

....
....
....
....

August 10

Dear God, today I am thankful for... | 20 ___

Dear God, today I am thankful for... | 20 ___

Dear God, today I am thankful for... | 20 ___

Dear God, today I am thankful for... | 20 ___

Dear God, today I am thankful for... | 20 ___

August 11

Dear God, today I am thankful for... | 20 ___

Dear God, today I am thankful for... | 20 ___

Dear God, today I am thankful for... | 20 ___

Dear God, today I am thankful for... | 20 ___

Dear God, today I am thankful for... | 20 ___

August 12

Dear God, today I am thankful for... | 20 ___

Dear God, today I am thankful for... | 20 ___

Dear God, today I am thankful for... | 20 ___

Dear God, today I am thankful for... | 20 ___

Dear God, today I am thankful for... | 20 ___

August 13

Dear God, today I am thankful for... | 20 ___

Dear God, today I am thankful for... | 20 ___

Dear God, today I am thankful for... | 20 ___

Dear God, today I am thankful for... | 20 ___

Dear God, today I am thankful for... | 20 ___

August 14

Dear God, today I am thankful for...   20 ___

Dear God, today I am thankful for...   20 ___

Dear God, today I am thankful for...   20 ___

Dear God, today I am thankful for...   20 ___

Dear God, today I am thankful for...   20 ___

August 15

Dear God, today I am thankful for... | 20 ___

Dear God, today I am thankful for... | 20 ___

Dear God, today I am thankful for... | 20 ___

Dear God, today I am thankful for... | 20 ___

Dear God, today I am thankful for... | 20 ___

August 16

Dear God, today I am thankful for... 20 ___

Dear God, today I am thankful for... 20 ___

Dear God, today I am thankful for... 20 ___

Dear God, today I am thankful for... 20 ___

Dear God, today I am thankful for... 20 ___

August 17

Dear God, today I am thankful for... | 20 ___

Dear God, today I am thankful for... | 20 ___

Dear God, today I am thankful for... | 20 ___

Dear God, today I am thankful for... | 20 ___

Dear God, today I am thankful for... | 20 ___

August 18

Dear God, today I am thankful for... | 20 ___

Dear God, today I am thankful for... | 20 ___

Dear God, today I am thankful for... | 20 ___

Dear God, today I am thankful for... | 20 ___

Dear God, today I am thankful for... | 20 ___

August 19

Dear God, today I am thankful for... | 20 ___

Dear God, today I am thankful for... | 20 ___

Dear God, today I am thankful for... | 20 ___

Dear God, today I am thankful for... | 20 ___

Dear God, today I am thankful for... | 20 ___

August 20

Dear God, today I am thankful for... | 20 ___

Dear God, today I am thankful for... | 20 ___

Dear God, today I am thankful for... | 20 ___

Dear God, today I am thankful for... | 20 ___

Dear God, today I am thankful for... | 20 ___

August 21

Dear God, today I am thankful for... | 20 ___

Dear God, today I am thankful for... | 20 ___

Dear God, today I am thankful for... | 20 ___

Dear God, today I am thankful for... | 20 ___

Dear God, today I am thankful for... | 20 ___

August 22

Dear God, today I am thankful for... | 20 ___

Dear God, today I am thankful for... | 20 ___

Dear God, today I am thankful for... | 20 ___

Dear God, today I am thankful for... | 20 ___

Dear God, today I am thankful for... | 20 ___

August 23

Dear God, today I am thankful for... | 20 ___

Dear God, today I am thankful for... | 20 ___

Dear God, today I am thankful for... | 20 ___

Dear God, today I am thankful for... | 20 ___

Dear God, today I am thankful for... | 20 ___

August 24

Dear God, today I am thankful for... | 20 ___

Dear God, today I am thankful for... | 20 ___

Dear God, today I am thankful for... | 20 ___

Dear God, today I am thankful for... | 20 ___

Dear God, today I am thankful for... | 20 ___

August 25

Dear God, today I am thankful for... | 20 ___

Dear God, today I am thankful for... | 20 ___

Dear God, today I am thankful for... | 20 ___

Dear God, today I am thankful for... | 20 ___

Dear God, today I am thankful for... | 20 ___

August 26

Dear God, today I am thankful for... | 20 ___

Dear God, today I am thankful for... | 20 ___

Dear God, today I am thankful for... | 20 ___

Dear God, today I am thankful for... | 20 ___

Dear God, today I am thankful for... | 20 ___

August 27

Dear God, today I am thankful for... | 20 ___

Dear God, today I am thankful for... | 20 ___

Dear God, today I am thankful for... | 20 ___

Dear God, today I am thankful for... | 20 ___

Dear God, today I am thankful for... | 20 ___

August 28

Dear God, today I am thankful for... | 20 ___

Dear God, today I am thankful for... | 20 ___

Dear God, today I am thankful for... | 20 ___

Dear God, today I am thankful for... | 20 ___

Dear God, today I am thankful for... | 20 ___

August 29

Dear God, today I am thankful for...   20 ___

Dear God, today I am thankful for...   20 ___

Dear God, today I am thankful for...   20 ___

Dear God, today I am thankful for...   20 ___

Dear God, today I am thankful for...   20 ___

August 30

Dear God, today I am thankful for... | 20 ___

Dear God, today I am thankful for... | 20 ___

Dear God, today I am thankful for... | 20 ___

Dear God, today I am thankful for... | 20 ___

Dear God, today I am thankful for... | 20 ___

August 31

Dear God, today I am thankful for... | 20 ___

Dear God, today I am thankful for... | 20 ___

Dear God, today I am thankful for... | 20 ___

Dear God, today I am thankful for... | 20 ___

Dear God, today I am thankful for... | 20 ___

September 1

Dear God, today I am thankful for... | 20 ___

Dear God, today I am thankful for... | 20 ___

Dear God, today I am thankful for... | 20 ___

Dear God, today I am thankful for... | 20 ___

Dear God, today I am thankful for... | 20 ___

September 2

Dear God, today I am thankful for... | 20 ___

Dear God, today I am thankful for... | 20 ___

Dear God, today I am thankful for... | 20 ___

Dear God, today I am thankful for... | 20 ___

Dear God, today I am thankful for... | 20 ___

September 3

Dear God, today I am thankful for... | 20 ___

Dear God, today I am thankful for... | 20 ___

Dear God, today I am thankful for... | 20 ___

Dear God, today I am thankful for... | 20 ___

Dear God, today I am thankful for... | 20 ___

September 4

Dear God, today I am thankful for... | 20 ___

Dear God, today I am thankful for... | 20 ___

Dear God, today I am thankful for... | 20 ___

Dear God, today I am thankful for... | 20 ___

Dear God, today I am thankful for... | 20 ___

September 5

Dear God, today I am thankful for...	20 ___

Dear God, today I am thankful for...	20 ___

Dear God, today I am thankful for...	20 ___

Dear God, today I am thankful for...	20 ___

Dear God, today I am thankful for...	20 ___

September 6

Dear God, today I am thankful for... | 20 ___

Dear God, today I am thankful for... | 20 ___

Dear God, today I am thankful for... | 20 ___

Dear God, today I am thankful for... | 20 ___

Dear God, today I am thankful for... | 20 ___

September 7

Dear God, today I am thankful for... | 20 ___

Dear God, today I am thankful for... | 20 ___

Dear God, today I am thankful for... | 20 ___

Dear God, today I am thankful for... | 20 ___

Dear God, today I am thankful for... | 20 ___

September 8

Dear God, today I am thankful for... | 20 ___

Dear God, today I am thankful for... | 20 ___

Dear God, today I am thankful for... | 20 ___

Dear God, today I am thankful for... | 20 ___

Dear God, today I am thankful for... | 20 ___

September 9

Dear God, today I am thankful for...   20 ___

Dear God, today I am thankful for...   20 ___

Dear God, today I am thankful for...   20 ___

Dear God, today I am thankful for...   20 ___

Dear God, today I am thankful for...   20 ___

September 10

Dear God, today I am thankful for... | 20 ___

Dear God, today I am thankful for... | 20 ___

Dear God, today I am thankful for... | 20 ___

Dear God, today I am thankful for... | 20 ___

Dear God, today I am thankful for... | 20 ___

September 11

| Dear God, today I am thankful for... | 20 ___ |

....
....
....
....

| Dear God, today I am thankful for... | 20 ___ |

....
....
....
....

| Dear God, today I am thankful for... | 20 ___ |

....
....
....
....

| Dear God, today I am thankful for... | 20 ___ |

....
....
....
....

| Dear God, today I am thankful for... | 20 ___ |

....
....
....
....

September 12

| Dear God, today I am thankful for... | 20 ___ |

| Dear God, today I am thankful for... | 20 ___ |

| Dear God, today I am thankful for... | 20 ___ |

| Dear God, today I am thankful for... | 20 ___ |

| Dear God, today I am thankful for... | 20 ___ |

September 13

Dear God, today I am thankful for… | 20 ___

Dear God, today I am thankful for… | 20 ___

Dear God, today I am thankful for… | 20 ___

Dear God, today I am thankful for… | 20 ___

Dear God, today I am thankful for… | 20 ___

September 14

| Dear God, today I am thankful for... | 20 ___ |

| Dear God, today I am thankful for... | 20 ___ |

| Dear God, today I am thankful for... | 20 ___ |

| Dear God, today I am thankful for... | 20 ___ |

| Dear God, today I am thankful for... | 20 ___ |

September 15

Dear God, today I am thankful for... | 20 ___

Dear God, today I am thankful for... | 20 ___

Dear God, today I am thankful for... | 20 ___

Dear God, today I am thankful for... | 20 ___

Dear God, today I am thankful for... | 20 ___

September 16

Dear God, today I am thankful for... | 20 ___

Dear God, today I am thankful for... | 20 ___

Dear God, today I am thankful for... | 20 ___

Dear God, today I am thankful for... | 20 ___

Dear God, today I am thankful for... | 20 ___

September 17

Dear God, today I am thankful for...   20 ___

....
....
....
....

Dear God, today I am thankful for...   20 ___

....
....
....
....

Dear God, today I am thankful for...   20 ___

....
....
....
....

Dear God, today I am thankful for...   20 ___

....
....
....
....

Dear God, today I am thankful for...   20 ___

....
....
....
....

September 18

Dear God, today I am thankful for... | 20 ___

Dear God, today I am thankful for... | 20 ___

Dear God, today I am thankful for... | 20 ___

Dear God, today I am thankful for... | 20 ___

Dear God, today I am thankful for... | 20 ___

September 19

Dear God, today I am thankful for... | 20 ___

Dear God, today I am thankful for... | 20 ___

Dear God, today I am thankful for... | 20 ___

Dear God, today I am thankful for... | 20 ___

Dear God, today I am thankful for... | 20 ___

September 20

Dear God, today I am thankful for...	20 ___

Dear God, today I am thankful for...	20 ___

Dear God, today I am thankful for...	20 ___

Dear God, today I am thankful for...	20 ___

Dear God, today I am thankful for...	20 ___

September 21

Dear God, today I am thankful for... | 20 ___

Dear God, today I am thankful for... | 20 ___

Dear God, today I am thankful for... | 20 ___

Dear God, today I am thankful for... | 20 ___

Dear God, today I am thankful for... | 20 ___

September 22

Dear God, today I am thankful for...   20 ___

....
....
....
....

Dear God, today I am thankful for...   20 ___

....
....
....
....

Dear God, today I am thankful for...   20 ___

....
....
....
....

Dear God, today I am thankful for...   20 ___

....
....
....
....

Dear God, today I am thankful for...   20 ___

....
....
....
....

September 23

Dear God, today I am thankful for... | 20 ___

Dear God, today I am thankful for... | 20 ___

Dear God, today I am thankful for... | 20 ___

Dear God, today I am thankful for... | 20 ___

Dear God, today I am thankful for... | 20 ___

September 24

| Dear God, today I am thankful for... | 20 ___ |

| Dear God, today I am thankful for... | 20 ___ |

| Dear God, today I am thankful for... | 20 ___ |

| Dear God, today I am thankful for... | 20 ___ |

| Dear God, today I am thankful for... | 20 ___ |

September 25

Dear God, today I am thankful for... | 20 ___

Dear God, today I am thankful for... | 20 ___

Dear God, today I am thankful for... | 20 ___

Dear God, today I am thankful for... | 20 ___

Dear God, today I am thankful for... | 20 ___

September 26

Dear God, today I am thankful for...   20 ___

Dear God, today I am thankful for...   20 ___

Dear God, today I am thankful for...   20 ___

Dear God, today I am thankful for...   20 ___

Dear God, today I am thankful for...   20 ___

September 27

| Dear God, today I am thankful for... | 20 ___ |

....

....

....

....

| Dear God, today I am thankful for... | 20 ___ |

....

....

....

....

| Dear God, today I am thankful for... | 20 ___ |

....

....

....

....

| Dear God, today I am thankful for... | 20 ___ |

....

....

....

....

| Dear God, today I am thankful for... | 20 ___ |

....

....

....

....

September 28

Dear God, today I am thankful for... | 20 ___

Dear God, today I am thankful for... | 20 ___

Dear God, today I am thankful for... | 20 ___

Dear God, today I am thankful for... | 20 ___

Dear God, today I am thankful for... | 20 ___

September 29

Dear God, today I am thankful for... | 20 ___

Dear God, today I am thankful for... | 20 ___

Dear God, today I am thankful for... | 20 ___

Dear God, today I am thankful for... | 20 ___

Dear God, today I am thankful for... | 20 ___

September 30

Dear God, today I am thankful for… | 20 ___

Dear God, today I am thankful for… | 20 ___

Dear God, today I am thankful for… | 20 ___

Dear God, today I am thankful for… | 20 ___

Dear God, today I am thankful for… | 20 ___

October 1

Dear God, today I am thankful for...   20 ___

Dear God, today I am thankful for...   20 ___

Dear God, today I am thankful for...   20 ___

Dear God, today I am thankful for...   20 ___

Dear God, today I am thankful for...   20 ___

October 2

Dear God, today I am thankful for... 20 ___

Dear God, today I am thankful for... 20 ___

Dear God, today I am thankful for... 20 ___

Dear God, today I am thankful for... 20 ___

Dear God, today I am thankful for... 20 ___

October 3

| Dear God, today I am thankful for... | 20 ___ |

| Dear God, today I am thankful for... | 20 ___ |

| Dear God, today I am thankful for... | 20 ___ |

| Dear God, today I am thankful for... | 20 ___ |

| Dear God, today I am thankful for... | 20 ___ |

October 4

Dear God, today I am thankful for... | 20 ____

Dear God, today I am thankful for... | 20 ____

Dear God, today I am thankful for... | 20 ____

Dear God, today I am thankful for... | 20 ____

Dear God, today I am thankful for... | 20 ____

October 5

Dear God, today I am thankful for...   20 ___

Dear God, today I am thankful for...   20 ___

Dear God, today I am thankful for...   20 ___

Dear God, today I am thankful for...   20 ___

Dear God, today I am thankful for...   20 ___

October 6

Dear God, today I am thankful for... | 20 ___

Dear God, today I am thankful for... | 20 ___

Dear God, today I am thankful for... | 20 ___

Dear God, today I am thankful for... | 20 ___

Dear God, today I am thankful for... | 20 ___

October 7

Dear God, today I am thankful for... | 20 ___

....
....
....

Dear God, today I am thankful for... | 20 ___

....
....
....

Dear God, today I am thankful for... | 20 ___

....
....
....

Dear God, today I am thankful for... | 20 ___

....
....
....

Dear God, today I am thankful for... | 20 ___

....
....
....

October 8

Dear God, today I am thankful for... | 20 ___

Dear God, today I am thankful for... | 20 ___

Dear God, today I am thankful for... | 20 ___

Dear God, today I am thankful for... | 20 ___

Dear God, today I am thankful for... | 20 ___

October 9

Dear God, today I am thankful for...	20 ___

Dear God, today I am thankful for...	20 ___

Dear God, today I am thankful for...	20 ___

Dear God, today I am thankful for...	20 ___

Dear God, today I am thankful for...	20 ___

October 10

Dear God, today I am thankful for... | 20 ___

Dear God, today I am thankful for... | 20 ___

Dear God, today I am thankful for... | 20 ___

Dear God, today I am thankful for... | 20 ___

Dear God, today I am thankful for... | 20 ___

October 11

Dear God, today I am thankful for... | 20 ___

Dear God, today I am thankful for... | 20 ___

Dear God, today I am thankful for... | 20 ___

Dear God, today I am thankful for... | 20 ___

Dear God, today I am thankful for... | 20 ___

October 12

Dear God, today I am thankful for... | 20 ___

Dear God, today I am thankful for... | 20 ___

Dear God, today I am thankful for... | 20 ___

Dear God, today I am thankful for... | 20 ___

Dear God, today I am thankful for... | 20 ___

October 13

Dear God, today I am thankful for...	20 ___

Dear God, today I am thankful for...	20 ___

Dear God, today I am thankful for...	20 ___

Dear God, today I am thankful for...	20 ___

Dear God, today I am thankful for...	20 ___

October 14

Dear God, today I am thankful for... | 20 ___

Dear God, today I am thankful for... | 20 ___

Dear God, today I am thankful for... | 20 ___

Dear God, today I am thankful for... | 20 ___

Dear God, today I am thankful for... | 20 ___

October 15

Dear God, today I am thankful for... | 20 ___

Dear God, today I am thankful for... | 20 ___

Dear God, today I am thankful for... | 20 ___

Dear God, today I am thankful for... | 20 ___

Dear God, today I am thankful for... | 20 ___

October 16

Dear God, today I am thankful for... | 20 ___

Dear God, today I am thankful for... | 20 ___

Dear God, today I am thankful for... | 20 ___

Dear God, today I am thankful for... | 20 ___

Dear God, today I am thankful for... | 20 ___

October 17

Dear God, today I am thankful for...	20 ___

Dear God, today I am thankful for...	20 ___

Dear God, today I am thankful for...	20 ___

Dear God, today I am thankful for...	20 ___

Dear God, today I am thankful for...	20 ___

October 18

Dear God, today I am thankful for... 20 ___

Dear God, today I am thankful for... 20 ___

Dear God, today I am thankful for... 20 ___

Dear God, today I am thankful for... 20 ___

Dear God, today I am thankful for... 20 ___

October 19

| Dear God, today I am thankful for… | 20 ___ |

....
....
....
....

| Dear God, today I am thankful for… | 20 ___ |

....
....
....
....

| Dear God, today I am thankful for… | 20 ___ |

....
....
....
....

| Dear God, today I am thankful for… | 20 ___ |

....
....
....
....

| Dear God, today I am thankful for… | 20 ___ |

....
....
....
....

October 20

Dear God, today I am thankful for... | 20 ___

Dear God, today I am thankful for... | 20 ___

Dear God, today I am thankful for... | 20 ___

Dear God, today I am thankful for... | 20 ___

Dear God, today I am thankful for... | 20 ___

October 21

Dear God, today I am thankful for... | 20 ___

Dear God, today I am thankful for... | 20 ___

Dear God, today I am thankful for... | 20 ___

Dear God, today I am thankful for... | 20 ___

Dear God, today I am thankful for... | 20 ___

October 22

Dear God, today I am thankful for... | 20 ___

Dear God, today I am thankful for... | 20 ___

Dear God, today I am thankful for... | 20 ___

Dear God, today I am thankful for... | 20 ___

Dear God, today I am thankful for... | 20 ___

October 23

Dear God, today I am thankful for... | 20 ___

....
....
....
....

Dear God, today I am thankful for... | 20 ___

....
....
....
....

Dear God, today I am thankful for... | 20 ___

....
....
....
....

Dear God, today I am thankful for... | 20 ___

....
....
....
....

Dear God, today I am thankful for... | 20 ___

....
....
....
....

October 24

Dear God, today I am thankful for... 20 ___

Dear God, today I am thankful for... 20 ___

Dear God, today I am thankful for... 20 ___

Dear God, today I am thankful for... 20 ___

Dear God, today I am thankful for... 20 ___

October 25

| Dear God, today I am thankful for... | 20 ___ |

| Dear God, today I am thankful for... | 20 ___ |

| Dear God, today I am thankful for... | 20 ___ |

| Dear God, today I am thankful for... | 20 ___ |

| Dear God, today I am thankful for... | 20 ___ |

October 26

Dear God, today I am thankful for...	20 ___

Dear God, today I am thankful for...	20 ___

Dear God, today I am thankful for...	20 ___

Dear God, today I am thankful for...	20 ___

Dear God, today I am thankful for...	20 ___

October 27

Dear God, today I am thankful for...	20 ___

Dear God, today I am thankful for...	20 ___

Dear God, today I am thankful for...	20 ___

Dear God, today I am thankful for...	20 ___

Dear God, today I am thankful for...	20 ___

October 28

Dear God, today I am thankful for... | 20 ___

Dear God, today I am thankful for... | 20 ___

Dear God, today I am thankful for... | 20 ___

Dear God, today I am thankful for... | 20 ___

Dear God, today I am thankful for... | 20 ___

October 29

Dear God, today I am thankful for...   20 ___

....
....
....
....

Dear God, today I am thankful for...   20 ___

....
....
....
....

Dear God, today I am thankful for...   20 ___

....
....
....
....

Dear God, today I am thankful for...   20 ___

....
....
....
....

Dear God, today I am thankful for...   20 ___

....
....
....
....

October 30

Dear God, today I am thankful for... | 20 ___

Dear God, today I am thankful for... | 20 ___

Dear God, today I am thankful for... | 20 ___

Dear God, today I am thankful for... | 20 ___

Dear God, today I am thankful for... | 20 ___

October 31

Dear God, today I am thankful for... | 20 ___

Dear God, today I am thankful for... | 20 ___

Dear God, today I am thankful for... | 20 ___

Dear God, today I am thankful for... | 20 ___

Dear God, today I am thankful for... | 20 ___

November 1

Dear God, today I am thankful for...	20 ___

Dear God, today I am thankful for...	20 ___

Dear God, today I am thankful for...	20 ___

Dear God, today I am thankful for...	20 ___

Dear God, today I am thankful for...	20 ___

November 2

Dear God, today I am thankful for...   20 ___

Dear God, today I am thankful for...   20 ___

Dear God, today I am thankful for...   20 ___

Dear God, today I am thankful for...   20 ___

Dear God, today I am thankful for...   20 ___

November 3

Dear God, today I am thankful for... | 20 ___

Dear God, today I am thankful for... | 20 ___

Dear God, today I am thankful for... | 20 ___

Dear God, today I am thankful for... | 20 ___

Dear God, today I am thankful for... | 20 ___

November 4

Dear God, today I am thankful for... | 20 ___

....
....
....
....

Dear God, today I am thankful for... | 20 ___

....
....
....
....

Dear God, today I am thankful for... | 20 ___

....
....
....
....

Dear God, today I am thankful for... | 20 ___

....
....
....
....

Dear God, today I am thankful for... | 20 ___

....
....
....
....

November 5

Dear God, today I am thankful for... | 20 ___

Dear God, today I am thankful for... | 20 ___

Dear God, today I am thankful for... | 20 ___

Dear God, today I am thankful for... | 20 ___

Dear God, today I am thankful for... | 20 ___

November 6

Dear God, today I am thankful for... | 20 ___

Dear God, today I am thankful for... | 20 ___

Dear God, today I am thankful for... | 20 ___

Dear God, today I am thankful for... | 20 ___

Dear God, today I am thankful for... | 20 ___

November 7

Dear God, today I am thankful for...	20 ___

Dear God, today I am thankful for...	20 ___

Dear God, today I am thankful for...	20 ___

Dear God, today I am thankful for...	20 ___

Dear God, today I am thankful for...	20 ___

November 8

Dear God, today I am thankful for... | 20 ___

Dear God, today I am thankful for... | 20 ___

Dear God, today I am thankful for... | 20 ___

Dear God, today I am thankful for... | 20 ___

Dear God, today I am thankful for... | 20 ___

November 9

Dear God, today I am thankful for... | 20 ___

Dear God, today I am thankful for... | 20 ___

Dear God, today I am thankful for... | 20 ___

Dear God, today I am thankful for... | 20 ___

Dear God, today I am thankful for... | 20 ___

November 10

| Dear God, today I am thankful for... | 20 ___ |

| Dear God, today I am thankful for... | 20 ___ |

| Dear God, today I am thankful for... | 20 ___ |

| Dear God, today I am thankful for... | 20 ___ |

| Dear God, today I am thankful for... | 20 ___ |

November 11

Dear God, today I am thankful for... | 20 ___

Dear God, today I am thankful for... | 20 ___

Dear God, today I am thankful for... | 20 ___

Dear God, today I am thankful for... | 20 ___

Dear God, today I am thankful for... | 20 ___

November 12

Dear God, today I am thankful for... | 20 ___

Dear God, today I am thankful for... | 20 ___

Dear God, today I am thankful for... | 20 ___

Dear God, today I am thankful for... | 20 ___

Dear God, today I am thankful for... | 20 ___

November 13

Dear God, today I am thankful for... | 20 ___

Dear God, today I am thankful for... | 20 ___

Dear God, today I am thankful for... | 20 ___

Dear God, today I am thankful for... | 20 ___

Dear God, today I am thankful for... | 20 ___

November 14

Dear God, today I am thankful for... | 20 ___

Dear God, today I am thankful for... | 20 ___

Dear God, today I am thankful for... | 20 ___

Dear God, today I am thankful for... | 20 ___

Dear God, today I am thankful for... | 20 ___

November 15

Dear God, today I am thankful for...   20 ___

Dear God, today I am thankful for...   20 ___

Dear God, today I am thankful for...   20 ___

Dear God, today I am thankful for...   20 ___

Dear God, today I am thankful for...   20 ___

November 16

Dear God, today I am thankful for... | 20 ___

Dear God, today I am thankful for... | 20 ___

Dear God, today I am thankful for... | 20 ___

Dear God, today I am thankful for... | 20 ___

Dear God, today I am thankful for... | 20 ___

November 17

Dear God, today I am thankful for...	20 ___

Dear God, today I am thankful for...	20 ___

Dear God, today I am thankful for...	20 ___

Dear God, today I am thankful for...	20 ___

Dear God, today I am thankful for...	20 ___

November 18

Dear God, today I am thankful for... | 20 ___

Dear God, today I am thankful for... | 20 ___

Dear God, today I am thankful for... | 20 ___

Dear God, today I am thankful for... | 20 ___

Dear God, today I am thankful for... | 20 ___

November 19

Dear God, today I am thankful for...	20 ___

Dear God, today I am thankful for...	20 ___

Dear God, today I am thankful for...	20 ___

Dear God, today I am thankful for...	20 ___

Dear God, today I am thankful for...	20 ___

November 20

Dear God, today I am thankful for... | 20 ___

....
....
....
....

Dear God, today I am thankful for... | 20 ___

....
....
....
....

Dear God, today I am thankful for... | 20 ___

....
....
....
....

Dear God, today I am thankful for... | 20 ___

....
....
....
....

Dear God, today I am thankful for... | 20 ___

....
....
....
....

November 21

Dear God, today I am thankful for... | 20 ___

Dear God, today I am thankful for... | 20 ___

Dear God, today I am thankful for... | 20 ___

Dear God, today I am thankful for... | 20 ___

Dear God, today I am thankful for... | 20 ___

November 22

Dear God, today I am thankful for... | 20 ___

Dear God, today I am thankful for... | 20 ___

Dear God, today I am thankful for... | 20 ___

Dear God, today I am thankful for... | 20 ___

Dear God, today I am thankful for... | 20 ___

November 23

Dear God, today I am thankful for…	20 ___

Dear God, today I am thankful for…	20 ___

Dear God, today I am thankful for…	20 ___

Dear God, today I am thankful for…	20 ___

Dear God, today I am thankful for…	20 ___

November 24

Dear God, today I am thankful for... | 20 ___

....
....
....

Dear God, today I am thankful for... | 20 ___

....
....
....

Dear God, today I am thankful for... | 20 ___

....
....
....

Dear God, today I am thankful for... | 20 ___

....
....
....

Dear God, today I am thankful for... | 20 ___

....
....
....

November 25

Dear God, today I am thankful for...	20 ___

Dear God, today I am thankful for...	20 ___

Dear God, today I am thankful for...	20 ___

Dear God, today I am thankful for...	20 ___

Dear God, today I am thankful for...	20 ___

November 26

Dear God, today I am thankful for...   20 ___

Dear God, today I am thankful for...   20 ___

Dear God, today I am thankful for...   20 ___

Dear God, today I am thankful for...   20 ___

Dear God, today I am thankful for...   20 ___

November 27

| Dear God, today I am thankful for... | 20 ___ |

| Dear God, today I am thankful for... | 20 ___ |

| Dear God, today I am thankful for... | 20 ___ |

| Dear God, today I am thankful for... | 20 ___ |

| Dear God, today I am thankful for... | 20 ___ |

November 28

Dear God, today I am thankful for... | 20 ___

Dear God, today I am thankful for... | 20 ___

Dear God, today I am thankful for... | 20 ___

Dear God, today I am thankful for... | 20 ___

Dear God, today I am thankful for... | 20 ___

November 29

Dear God, today I am thankful for... | 20 ___

Dear God, today I am thankful for... | 20 ___

Dear God, today I am thankful for... | 20 ___

Dear God, today I am thankful for... | 20 ___

Dear God, today I am thankful for... | 20 ___

November 30

Dear God, today I am thankful for... | 20 ___

Dear God, today I am thankful for... | 20 ___

Dear God, today I am thankful for... | 20 ___

Dear God, today I am thankful for... | 20 ___

Dear God, today I am thankful for... | 20 ___

December 1

| Dear God, today I am thankful for... | 20 ___ |

....
....
....
....

| Dear God, today I am thankful for... | 20 ___ |

....
....
....
....

| Dear God, today I am thankful for... | 20 ___ |

....
....
....
....

| Dear God, today I am thankful for... | 20 ___ |

....
....
....
....

| Dear God, today I am thankful for... | 20 ___ |

....
....
....
....

December 2

| Dear God, today I am thankful for... | 20 ___ |

| Dear God, today I am thankful for... | 20 ___ |

| Dear God, today I am thankful for... | 20 ___ |

| Dear God, today I am thankful for... | 20 ___ |

| Dear God, today I am thankful for... | 20 ___ |

December 3

| Dear God, today I am thankful for... | 20 ___ |

....
....
....
....

| Dear God, today I am thankful for... | 20 ___ |

....
....
....
....

| Dear God, today I am thankful for... | 20 ___ |

....
....
....
....

| Dear God, today I am thankful for... | 20 ___ |

....
....
....
....

| Dear God, today I am thankful for... | 20 ___ |

....
....
....
....

December 4

Dear God, today I am thankful for... | 20 ___

Dear God, today I am thankful for... | 20 ___

Dear God, today I am thankful for... | 20 ___

Dear God, today I am thankful for... | 20 ___

Dear God, today I am thankful for... | 20 ___

December 5

Dear God, today I am thankful for... | 20 ___

Dear God, today I am thankful for... | 20 ___

Dear God, today I am thankful for... | 20 ___

Dear God, today I am thankful for... | 20 ___

Dear God, today I am thankful for... | 20 ___

December 6

Dear God, today I am thankful for...	20 ___

Dear God, today I am thankful for...	20 ___

Dear God, today I am thankful for...	20 ___

Dear God, today I am thankful for...	20 ___

Dear God, today I am thankful for...	20 ___

December 7

Dear God, today I am thankful for...	20 ___

Dear God, today I am thankful for...	20 ___

Dear God, today I am thankful for...	20 ___

Dear God, today I am thankful for...	20 ___

Dear God, today I am thankful for...	20 ___

December 8

| Dear God, today I am thankful for... | 20 ___ |

| Dear God, today I am thankful for... | 20 ___ |

| Dear God, today I am thankful for... | 20 ___ |

| Dear God, today I am thankful for... | 20 ___ |

| Dear God, today I am thankful for... | 20 ___ |

December 9

Dear God, today I am thankful for... | 20 ___

Dear God, today I am thankful for... | 20 ___

Dear God, today I am thankful for... | 20 ___

Dear God, today I am thankful for... | 20 ___

Dear God, today I am thankful for... | 20 ___

December 10

Dear God, today I am thankful for... | 20 ___

Dear God, today I am thankful for... | 20 ___

Dear God, today I am thankful for... | 20 ___

Dear God, today I am thankful for... | 20 ___

Dear God, today I am thankful for... | 20 ___

December 11

Dear God, today I am thankful for... | 20 ___

Dear God, today I am thankful for... | 20 ___

Dear God, today I am thankful for... | 20 ___

Dear God, today I am thankful for... | 20 ___

Dear God, today I am thankful for... | 20 ___

December 12

Dear God, today I am thankful for... | 20 ___

Dear God, today I am thankful for... | 20 ___

Dear God, today I am thankful for... | 20 ___

Dear God, today I am thankful for... | 20 ___

Dear God, today I am thankful for... | 20 ___

December 13

Dear God, today I am thankful for... | 20 ___

Dear God, today I am thankful for... | 20 ___

Dear God, today I am thankful for... | 20 ___

Dear God, today I am thankful for... | 20 ___

Dear God, today I am thankful for... | 20 ___

December 14

Dear God, today I am thankful for...   20 ___

Dear God, today I am thankful for...   20 ___

Dear God, today I am thankful for...   20 ___

Dear God, today I am thankful for...   20 ___

Dear God, today I am thankful for...   20 ___

December 15

Dear God, today I am thankful for... | 20 ___

Dear God, today I am thankful for... | 20 ___

Dear God, today I am thankful for... | 20 ___

Dear God, today I am thankful for... | 20 ___

Dear God, today I am thankful for... | 20 ___

December 16

Dear God, today I am thankful for... | 20 ___

....
....
....
....

Dear God, today I am thankful for... | 20 ___

....
....
....
....

Dear God, today I am thankful for... | 20 ___

....
....
....
....

Dear God, today I am thankful for... | 20 ___

....
....
....
....

Dear God, today I am thankful for... | 20 ___

....
....
....
....

December 17

Dear God, today I am thankful for... | 20 ___

Dear God, today I am thankful for... | 20 ___

Dear God, today I am thankful for... | 20 ___

Dear God, today I am thankful for... | 20 ___

Dear God, today I am thankful for... | 20 ___

December 18

Dear God, today I am thankful for... | 20 ___

Dear God, today I am thankful for... | 20 ___

Dear God, today I am thankful for... | 20 ___

Dear God, today I am thankful for... | 20 ___

Dear God, today I am thankful for... | 20 ___

December 19

Dear God, today I am thankful for... | 20 ___

Dear God, today I am thankful for... | 20 ___

Dear God, today I am thankful for... | 20 ___

Dear God, today I am thankful for... | 20 ___

Dear God, today I am thankful for... | 20 ___

December 20

Dear God, today I am thankful for... | 20 ___

....
....
....

Dear God, today I am thankful for... | 20 ___

....
....
....

Dear God, today I am thankful for... | 20 ___

....
....
....

Dear God, today I am thankful for... | 20 ___

....
....
....

Dear God, today I am thankful for... | 20 ___

....
....
....

December 21

Dear God, today I am thankful for... | 20 ___

Dear God, today I am thankful for... | 20 ___

Dear God, today I am thankful for... | 20 ___

Dear God, today I am thankful for... | 20 ___

Dear God, today I am thankful for... | 20 ___

December 22

Dear God, today I am thankful for... | 20 ___

Dear God, today I am thankful for... | 20 ___

Dear God, today I am thankful for... | 20 ___

Dear God, today I am thankful for... | 20 ___

Dear God, today I am thankful for... | 20 ___

December 23

Dear God, today I am thankful for... 20 ___

Dear God, today I am thankful for... 20 ___

Dear God, today I am thankful for... 20 ___

Dear God, today I am thankful for... 20 ___

Dear God, today I am thankful for... 20 ___

December 24

Dear God, today I am thankful for...   20 ___

Dear God, today I am thankful for...   20 ___

Dear God, today I am thankful for...   20 ___

Dear God, today I am thankful for...   20 ___

Dear God, today I am thankful for...   20 ___

December 25

Dear God, today I am thankful for...   20 ___

Dear God, today I am thankful for...   20 ___

Dear God, today I am thankful for...   20 ___

Dear God, today I am thankful for...   20 ___

Dear God, today I am thankful for...   20 ___

December 26

Dear God, today I am thankful for...	20 ___

Dear God, today I am thankful for...	20 ___

Dear God, today I am thankful for...	20 ___

Dear God, today I am thankful for...	20 ___

Dear God, today I am thankful for...	20 ___

December 27

Dear God, today I am thankful for... 20 ___

Dear God, today I am thankful for... 20 ___

Dear God, today I am thankful for... 20 ___

Dear God, today I am thankful for... 20 ___

Dear God, today I am thankful for... 20 ___

December 28

Dear God, today I am thankful for... | 20 ___

Dear God, today I am thankful for... | 20 ___

Dear God, today I am thankful for... | 20 ___

Dear God, today I am thankful for... | 20 ___

Dear God, today I am thankful for... | 20 ___

December 29

Dear God, today I am thankful for... | 20 ___

Dear God, today I am thankful for... | 20 ___

Dear God, today I am thankful for... | 20 ___

Dear God, today I am thankful for... | 20 ___

Dear God, today I am thankful for... | 20 ___

December 30

Dear God, today I am thankful for...   20 ___

....
....
....

Dear God, today I am thankful for...   20 ___

....
....
....

Dear God, today I am thankful for...   20 ___

....
....
....

Dear God, today I am thankful for...   20 ___

....
....
....

Dear God, today I am thankful for...   20 ___

....
....
....

December 31

Dear God, today I am thankful for... | 20 ___

Dear God, today I am thankful for... | 20 ___

Dear God, today I am thankful for... | 20 ___

Dear God, today I am thankful for... | 20 ___

Dear God, today I am thankful for... | 20 ___

Keep Track Books brings you a variety
of essential journals and notebooks —
including gratitude journals
with the same interior as this one,
but with different cover designs.

Search for 'Keep Track Books' on Amazon
or visit www.lusciousbooks.co.uk
to discover more journals and notebooks.

Made in the USA
Monee, IL
07 November 2019